WORK, LAN
EDUCATION
INDUSTRIAL ЅTATE

GW01017791

by
Michael Duane

FREEDOM PRESS
London
1991

Published by
FREEDOM PRESS
84b Whitechapel High Street
London E1 7QX
1991

ISBN 0 900384 59 X

Printed and typeset in Great Britain by Aldgate Press, London E1 7QX

Contents

Prologue

'Today, the capitalist state is a 'Welfare State', the term being general-
ly used to designate that combination of economic and political
factors which characterize industrialized and non-socialist states.
Such a state is one in which an attempt is made to off-set the private
problems of health, education and economic well-being which are
produced by the 'free-market' economic system. The attempt to ame-
liorate the conditions of life is a response to the fact that the resources
provided to individuals on the labour market (in wages and salaries)
are not adequate to meet the costs of medical care, the education of
oneself and one's children, and the satisfaction of material needs
during periods of unemployment. These 'goods' are purchased in-
stead by the government and distributed to those who meet predeter-
mined administrative criteria. Thus the welfare state presents us with
an altruistic image of itself. It is given to us as a political system
which responds to the needs of its less fortunate members, as a
society in which the 'haves' are required to surrender some of their
wealth to the 'have-nots', as a state which directs some resources
towards ends which, though desirable, would not be sought if the
effective demand of private persons were the sole determinant of
economic decisions. It is also a fundamentally conservative image,
for it affirms the established order of politics and society, ascribing
virtue and necessity to the complicated bureaucratic pyramid of the
state grown large, as the boundaries of its presumed concerns and
competence have expanded.

The financing of the modern bureaucratic and welfare state has
involved state control of an increasingly large proportion of the
community's resources – through taxation, intervention, and even

state-ownership. Those reactionaries, found in the Tory parties of both Canada and the United Kingdon, and in both main American parties, who call themselves 'conservatives', and who would unburden the state of its economic holdings, are often concerned that economic incompetence and political oppression are the inevitable by-product of this trend. . . They are right. . . When the Conservative government of Britain sells off the state's controlling interest in a number of corporations . . . the goal is to replace state domination with the domination of private capital. The overpowering controls of the expanding state . . . is to be replaced by a reborn capitalism – according to the 'conservatives'. As such they promote myths of free-market efficiency and automatic economic equilibrium which are the identifying marks of 19th century liberalism (which is why they are better understood as reactionaries, looking backwards to some golden age of pre-interventionist economic freedom and harmony).'
                          The Modern State by Frank Harrison*

(* published by Black Rose Books, distributed by *Freedom Press*)

1
Work

The nature of work in industrial society today is such that those who stop to think about it wonder why so many millions of otherwise sane people spend so much of their lives, apparently without complaint, at work over which they have no control and from which they derive no personal satisfaction beyond receiving a wage. It is now a commonplace that although they make no complaint many suffer from impairment of health and sanity. The history of industrial work is the history of a long battle to secure levels of pay that would enable the workers and their families to live healthy and modestly comfortable lives; to limit the hours of work so as to have leisure and recreation outside working hours; and to work under conditions that avoid injuries, illnesses caused by the nature of the work and prolonged strain or exhaustion.

Types of work
In capitalist industrial society the type of work done varies from heavy, unskilled manual labour carried out under the detailed direction of a ganger or foreman and requiring a minimum of intellectual effort or personal responsibility, through a wide range of skilled manual or craft work, clerical work that may consist simply of routine filing, copy-typing, typing from taped dictation or brief notes, rising to very complicated calculations or the creative manipulation of facts, figures and possibilities, such as may be necessary for a lawyer's clerk. On the other hand work may be totally

creative and idiosyncratic, such as that of an artist or a novelist, or it may demand a long training combined with creative talent such as that used by outstanding mathematicians, scientists, teachers, barristers, administrators or psychoanalysts. The list of the different types of work and of the qualities that are demanded will vary with the technical sophistication of the society.

The Spectrum of Occupations

For the moment I will not look at the group of unemployed who now have become a permanent feature of industrialised societies and include members of all but the propertied group. Let us imagine that we take all those who work in our society and arrange them in a line with the least skilled at the left-hand end of the line, as we face it, and the most highly skilled at the right-hand end. For this purpose we will assume that skill is measured by the length of time and the cost of the education and training necessary for a particular skill. When we stand back and look at the line we will be likely to see at the left-hand end those whose work takes little or no training and no education beyond the most rudimentary our society provides. There will stand the charladies, the part-time cafe waitresses, casual labourers with little or no continuity of employment and, in general, those who receive the very lowest rates of pay. At the other end of the spectrum we shall see the most notable and the most wealthy of our public figures and their families, such as the Monarch, the landed nobility and those who combine very great riches with positions of power, whether monetary or political. Power and wealth usually go together in Britain: it is rare to find that a really powerful figure is not very rich and vice versa.

Close to the nobility and near to the right-hand end of the spectrum are found those at the tops of their professions – judges and leading barristers; Vice-chancellors of the major universities (Chancellors are usually members of the Royal Family or senior members of the nobility or, in other universities, elder statesmen). Then come eminent scientists, leading figures from the armed forces with experience in the War Office, from the Bank of England, especially with experience of international banking; leaders from the biggest national-ised and private international and national corporations and top civil servants. A little to their left come the older professions – medicine, law, the Church, professors of older universities, and, in descending order, owners of and major shareholders and executives in large enterprises such as Marks and Spencer or British Airways, heads of Public Schools and Direct Grant Grammar schools and teachers in Oxbridge. In this region of the spectrum, power deriving directly from wealth and power from influence or position – as with senior government Ministers – overlaps. Many holders of public office, such as Ministers of State and many owners of large corporations also own large estates and farms run as businesses.

The owners of the press – the opinion formers – wield great power without responsibility, sometimes in a very destructive manner, as when they can deliberately set out to break the reputation or influence of any politician or public figure with whom they disagree, or boost, correspondingly, the reputation of those whom they favour or whom they seek to influence. The only curb on their influence is a drop in their circulation or a politically educated readership, so, like Murdoch, they constantly seek to broaden the base of their influence by buying up more and more papers, television channels and the sales outlets for their papers so as to extend their control. With new techniques in production some owners broke the power of the print unions by printing with greatly diminished manpower and bought the loyalty of the journalists with more pay – the Wapping dispute. They in-creased their power, but at the cost of having to buy up more and more small, local papers to keep in the lead. Murdoch owns papers, distributing agencies and shares in television in at least three continents. He has become, therefore, a real threat to democratic freedom of speech and publication.

Then come the semi-professions: teachers in state grammar schools, comprehensive schools and other secondary schools, primary schools and infant schools; nurses, social workers and a wide range of people with training according to recognised institutes. They may display very high degrees of skill and may work with people, as in psychotherapy, rather than with materials. A similar group of skilled people, also trained in recognised institutes, is made up of accountants, surveyors and so on.

Skilled manual workers appear in all industries and trades although automation has reduced their numbers in some industries such as car manufacture and brewing. They are trained through the apprenticeship system which itself has declined as new techniques have overtaken many traditional skills and because many skills in, for example, the building industry, are changing year by year through an increase in prefabrication and the use of new materials.

The semi-skilled category, closely tied as it was to the skilled category, has been eroded as a separate group and has merged with unskilled manual workers to form a large amorphous body of labour ready to turn its hand to anything under the control of technicians in the various trades. With large-scale unemployment this lowest section of the spectrum of occupations is constantly in and out of employment, picking up what expertise it can and, willy-nilly getting a degree of adaptability if not of specific skill.

Changes in Category
Over a period of years the spectrum of occupations does not remain rigid but displays a certain flux, particularly below the professional groups, as new materials and skills change and some jobs lose or gain importance. At the right-hand end of the spectrum there is obviously much more stability since this group has the power, based on wealth, to maintain their customs, traditions and style of life. The extreme example of flux is provided during periods of war when great changes take place both in the numbers of occupations held important enough to continue, and in the number of people retrained or diverted into other occupations, as, for example, into the manufacture of armaments and the draining of the

more junior ranks of the professions to provide the numbers for much enlarged forces. A post-war period usually sees changes within all occupations as people with new experience and different ideas return to civilian life.

Analysing the Spectrum

In a society as complex as industrial Britain our daily experience tells us that some people give orders and most have to obey them in order to minimise confusion. A close look at the different types of occupation represented on the spectrum will make clear where power and decision lie in this society, who obeys whatever orders are given and, further, who gives shape to those orders so that they are intelligible, not only in the sense that they can be understood but that they will co-ordinate with the myriads of other and different orders all being given continuously. For example, if war or a dispute over oil prices has led to a closure of oil fields so that rationing has to be imposed, who makes the order? Who ensures a fair distribution of petrol? Who decides that certain people such as doctors should get more petrol than others?. . . Parliament and the current government can decide that rationing is necessary but if action is to be taken the decision of Parliament has to be made known, penalties for breaking the new regulations must be fixed, schemes have to be set up to get the different qualities needed by different industries distributed in an orderly way, and so on.

Broadly speaking, there are three main groups spread across the spectrum: the first group, at the right-hand end, are those who by their ability to employ, command great political power, whether they get themselves elected to office within governments or not. Many choose to do so because they have thereby immediate access to the power to make certain decisions. Some choose to operate through the media so as to influence public opinion and, to that extent, make governments toe their particular line. One important function of the media, at least from the point of view of the wealthier section of society, is to reiterate the established values of the society so as to discourage any tendency towards revolution, and especially the tendency of workers to struggle for better pay and conditions of work. Wealth, of course, is not simply the possession of currency which itself can lose its value very quickly under certain conditions. Wealth is, in the classic formulation, 'the ownership of the means of production and distribution', namely, the land itself, factories, mines, oil, workshops, railways, roads, ships and waterways, and the people to operate them. It is because these entities produce more money than is needed for other costs or for wages that owners are rich.

The 'Ruling Class'

It is the 6 or 7 percent at the right-hand end of the spectrum who effectively control the destinies of our society. They do this through their public offices, their boards of directors, their political and financial committees and their influence on public opinion. Each member of one committee is also a member of a number of other parallel and related commit-tees. In this way a tight cohesion is maintained in what, on the surface, appears to be a loose and unco-ordinated assembly of organisations. And should there be any danger that the harmony between these organisations might be less than good, there is always the 'old boy' network. This system of relationships, so often derided by lesser mortals and the butt of innumerable jokes, has proved itself to have enduring strength, because it is made up of so many interwoven strands – financial, industrial and political interests; inter-marriage and emotional bonds first formed in the 'hothouse' atmosphere of the Public School, and the ultimate class and personal identity that results from the many and intense forms of socialisation that are directed at the young in the creation of an elite.

Now whereas the business meetings ensure that all the technical details are co-ordinated and that the professionals and their myriad clerks and underlings will carry decisions into action, the 'old boy' network operates through the Club, through the vast social ritual of the huntin', shootin' and fishin' calendar and through the long list of social events –

where one's absence would be the target of disapproving comment – to bind members into an even more effective cohesion. These social events, largely made up of house parties, formal and informal dinners and country-house weekends, serve to maintain the close personal knowledge essential for intuitive co-ordination in action and under stress. This tight unification into what is, effectively, a power elite, to use Wright Mills' phrase, makes the British Establishment or Ruling Class one of the most powerful in the world.

Among those immediately to the left of the owners of wealth are the 'managerial and professional groups', those who have the skills to manage the land, commerce and industry so well that they continue to earn money for the owners. They also invest in other enterprises at home and overseas so that no money remains idle but continues to accumulate more money at the fastest possible rate. Whatever the particular range of skills used by this group, their central and constant preoccupation is to protect and increase the wealth of their employers. Naturally, for this important task they are themselves very well paid and often, as a further incentive to do well and remain honest, they are granted high honours by the government of the day. Occasionally, however, a 'bad apple' uses his expertise to make a few quick bucks for himself, but the Niagara of abuse that is poured on him, as well as the enormous sums spent either in hushing the whole episode up so as to retain confidence in business, or in court fees to bring him to book, betrays the anxiety felt by the whole of this particular network at any breaking of their closely agreed regulations which are a vital part of their own self-protection.

It is from this area downwards that the effects of education are most powerfully felt on the spectrum of occupations. With expertise you can advance to higher positions to the point where the nobility and the landed gentry border on the higher ranks of the professionals. The 'ruling class' can always buy the expertise it needs, but one cannot so easily buy one's way into the very top. Into the Lords, perhaps, as a reward for political service or donations to Party funds, but usually only into that section of those who appear in the Lords only when summoned, as backwoodsmen, to prevent a Tory government being put in danger, or to prevent a wild Labour government dreaming of weakening the power of private property.

To the left of this group are the rather more obvious 'wage slaves', those who work or starve. They have no resources of wealth to fall back on because one of the central tenets of the owners of the means of production and distribution is to keep the work force paid as little as possible in the interests of 'cutting costs' in order to maximise their own wealth. A machine will break down and cease to create wealth if you neglect it, but a human being can be persuaded to work efficiently when his family is hungry or he burdened by excessive bills for rent or mortgage, because the alternative is unemployment. To that extent he is 'owned' by his employer. The drive to increase profits – 'greed made holy by business morality' – maintains through low wages a culture that is positively inhuman for the poorest section of our 'democracy'. Whatever education they may have picked up at home or in the few short years before leaving school for work or unemployment, they will not have been able to follow it up with books, ideas, art, argument, music or whatever for the simple reason that they have no money. To pay poor people enough to live in modest comfort would bring down the demon inflation on everyone – so runs the rubric. Hence the passion displayed whenever inflation threatens. But the real worry of those who are 'stinking rich' is that serious inflation might make them rather less rich. The arguments have little to do with the welfare of ordinary people who can barter their skills or set up their own small businesses at a fraction of the cost charged by bigger enterprises. A slump may not close factories but it does not rob the land of its fertility, so the landed gentry are secure despite minor inconveniences, even such troublesome ones as the English and the French revolutions, provided they keep their heads down, if not in the basket, for a while.

To revert for a moment to the question *why* people work for very low wages. We have to consider what life in an industrial town is like for those who are unemployed. Such towns are like deserts during working hours if you have no money to spend. The only companions you can have are your fellow-unemployed. Shops and pubs are not for the penniless; parks and recreation grounds may afford a break if the weather is fine; in winter you have to be well-clad and well-fed to enjoy them. If you are lucky you may find a church-hall that offers a free snack or a cup of tea, but they cannot encourage regular visitors because they do not have enough regular funds. The only thing to do, if you have no means of making money by doing odd jobs, is to spend the day in bed to conserve heating and avoid the temptation of wandering round the shops. People do not choose to be unemployed or idle because work – the application of skill to materials to satisfy a social need – is essential to our very wellbeing. It is a focus for talk either about the work itself or about our common interests. Those who believe that people are idle by nature are revelling in their own wishful thinking.

The Graph of Income
If we plot the graph of 'take-home pay', i.e. after income tax and national insurance, the line representing average income for each of the occupations (excluding the Monarchy) runs from, on the left, a low of under £100 for a forty-hour week, to a high on the right of over £10,000 for a week's 'work' (mostly performed by others) that permits, in working time, absence for social events such as Ascot, Henley, Goodwood, Wimbledon or whatever is the current engagement, with at least a month in the summer and generous breaks at Christmas and Easter. At that level of society how long one works or whether one works at all on a particular day is determined by business appointments and the social calendar. Deputies and secretarial staff cover most emergencies.

The figures quoted above were those obtaining in early 1990 but now under annual revision as new wage claims begin to arrive. These new claims seek to counter the effects of an inflation rate of nearly nine percent over the preceding year. This constant battle to maintain the purchasing power of wages is endemic to every capitalist economy where zero inflation is a dream never to be fulfilled for a wide variety of reasons that include the fact that armaments can not be used to plough the land or grow crops, and that masses of wealth in the form of money are transferred from many pockets into few simply by dealing on the money markets without corresponding results in goods or services.

The change in the different occupational levels of pay from left to right is not represented by a steady and even slope; it looks rather like a logarithmic curve in that the steepness of the curve increases as you move from left to right. There are some apparent anomalies as, for instance, that the average wage of the most skilled manual workers lies well above the average wage of office workers on fairly routine tasks. On the strict bases of skill as defined the lower grade office workers would fall somewhere near the semi-skilled manual group and not far from the charladies, but it is conventional to group together occupations which have a common basis in the types of skill used.

Ruling Class – Democracy?
Part of the reason for the success of the British ruling class in action lies in its 'charm', its 'reasonableness' and above all in the 'confidence' which it exudes by style of dress, behaviour, accent and the cultivated skill of never seeming to be at a loss. We shall look at this later when considering different patterns of socialisation in different types of home and school: at the way in which the natural confidence of young children is steadily eroded in the lower ranks of the nuclear family, and at the way in which an apparent confidence, that often appears as arrogance, is built into the upper social classes. To anyone who cares to look closely the underlying insecurity can be seen in particular forms of voice modulation and in certain styles of behaviour, gesture and facial expression under pressure. But more of this later.

A practical example of what I mean could be seen in William Whitelaw, appointed to 'solve' the problem of Ulster. When he left that post at the end of November 1973, he had neither solved nor come near to solving the political crisis, but his most entrenched opponents, left and right, were by then paying tribute to him as a 'man of integrity, reason and sincerity'. What he *had* done was to change the climate of opinion sufficiently to weaken the intensity and universality of support for the IRA among the Catholic population and, thereby, give time for the British troops to strengthen their positions and their counter-espionage. The change of opinion was brought about by the skilful way in which the trivial act of proposing to release hundreds of innocuous detainees was made to seem to be a major concession to the force of reasoned argument put forward by the SDLP and others.

The study of Whitelaw the public figure reveals how, first a man can be so saturated with the values of his class that he is indeed 'sincere'; so thoroughly educated in the politics and economics of power that his thinking is well-integrated and self-consistent and is, therefore 'reasonable'. He is, as a result, 'charming', i.e. he listens with care to everything, the better to understand it and to be in a position more effectively to reach the objectives with which he has set out. He has no need to be rude or brusque because he knows that he holds the ultimate power. That power was used when needed, but films showing British troops in action against civilians were banned from public showing. In modern 'democratic' forms of government Wright Mills' 'authority', 'manipulation' and 'coercion' are used as the government decides and 'the government' is the servant of the rich and powerful. We may be able to air most, if not all of our complaints in public; the fact remains that, in the end, he who holds power will get his way. And because those who hold the power also make the laws they have, as we shall see later, a certain kind of psychological stranglehold round the necks of their people.

2
Language

Work Roles and Linguistic Skills

As well as the disparity in income/wealth and political power
as between the ends of the spectrum of work, there is a third
factor of importance. It is the degree to which the various
categories of work require the exercise of linguistic skills on
the part of the worker for their successful performance –
linguistic skills being defined as skills in the manipulation or
comprehension of those systems of symbols – speech, writing,
mathematics, graphics and the other visual, tactile, auditory
or kinaesthetic systems used within our culture. This differ-
ence and the reasons for it can be more clearly seen if we
consider the work-role of the manual group as a whole and
that of the non-manual group as a whole. The manual group,
at whatever level of skill, is there to carry out the instructions
of the non-manual group, and to do so promptly and without
question because delay, as I hope to show presently, so often
spells loss of production and profit. The task of the non-
manual group, and especially the task of the professional,
managerial and property-owning sectors, is to direct, regulate
and control the whole economy on behalf of the owners.

Within the non-manual group as a whole this task is broken
down so that the general pattern of action or 'policy' is made
by the 6 or 7 percent at the right-hand of the spectrum, to
whom I have already referred. At some stage, sometimes
early in the process, sometimes much later, depending on

18

whether opposition is to be expected and whether, therefore, much work behind the scenes has to be done before the policy can be openly published, there is a process of 'sounding out' of ideas, carried out through the 'old boy' network, through articles in the more serious press by trusted journalists or lesser political figures to 'test the water'. Sometimes, if the issues are important enough there will be a nation-wide testing of feeling through the ranks of the party faithful. Memoirs of former Prime Ministers and their colleagues in Cabinet abound with examples of this kind. On it rests the claim that government in this country is 'democratic'. It resembles the 'democracy' that existed in the army when we were advancing across France after the invasion of Normandy. Since the advance was rapid it was necessary for the Corps and Divisional commanders to meet often in order to consolidate what had been gained and to continue the advance in an orderly manner. They would meet at a given point, the Chief-of-Staff of the Corps would review the situation and outline the next step. At this point the divisional commanders would put forward other suggestions for objectives, timing or methods and discussion would follow until there was general agreement. During this discussion they referred to one another, including their subordinate officers, as 'Dicky', or 'Hammer' or 'Pogo' – using the first names or nicknames they had used at their Public Schools. Later my own commander, Lieutenant-General Sir Richard O'Connor, then commanding The Eighth Armoured Corps, asked me, in some embarrassment, not to attend these meetings but to remain with the Scout cars in which we travelled. It appeared that the general commanding the Eleventh Armoured Division had discovered that I had not been educated at a Public school but at a Jesuit school and thought it unsuitable that a mere commoner should be present at the meetings of the generals. It was not that I was the most junior officer present. Our democracy, even today, fifty years afterwards, is like the democracy of Athens: it excludes the slaves. Since the definition of a slave is 'one who has to serve the purposes of another' there must be many slaves in Britain today, despite the efforts of Wilberforce.

I have referred to the fact that the central task of the professional and managerial group is to protect and increase the wealth of their masters. Since in the two hundred years between the Industrial Revolution and today the technical complexity of industry, banking, research, investment, exploration, the police, the armed forces and the other means by which we extend and protect wealth has increased beyond what was thought possible even just before the war, the skills and the language of management and the professions have changed greatly. Whereas at the time of Isambard Kingdom Brunel most middle-class people who were not engineers would have been able to read a technical description of his bridge at Saltash, today a technical description of the Channel Tunnel would have to be very loosely translated to be intelligible to the people who will use it. So the relatively simple language used by the ruling 6 percent has to be translated into the sets of technical instructions that will apply to banks, transport systems, police, insurance agents, trade unions, factories and laboratories, as well as to the press for transmission to the public in the styles favoured by the different newspapers.

Closely associated with the professions are the semi-professions who implement the work of the professions at an executive level and who identify with the values and objectives of the professions: nurses who carry out the instructions of surgeons and doctors; local government officials who apply the directives issued at Whitehall; grammar and comprehensive school teachers who apply the curricula set by the universities. . . Or they disseminate their instructions in forms intelligible to ordinary people, as when Town Hall clerks translate Whitehall building regulations for local builders, whereas building corporations employ their own lawyers to extract the maximum advantage from the same regulations.

The problem of 'Identification' and Subservience
'Identification' is a perfectly natural phenomenon that occurs

when people work together for common ends and build up a rapport through daily contact in cooperative work. In modern political, industrial and administrative practice it is commonly taken advantage of when 'dirty work' has to be done on behalf of the responsible senior partner in such a manner that the blame will not be attributed to him: he will be able to preserve the image of the benign and kindly employer even when he has to take unpopular decisions. The underling, anxious to please the boss, anticipates the need for the boss to give him a direct order to do the 'dirty work', so the boss can 'truthfully' say that he gave no order, if later challenged. The murder of Thomas a Becket is, of course, a classic example since the order was not directly given to De Tracey and his fellow murderers who loyally took the punishment from the Pope on the king's behalf.

'Subservience' is a different matter but can easily be the major part in a relationship between employer and employee, especially when the employee is almost completely, if not completely dependent for work and payment on that employer. This dependency is a direct result of the removal of land and property from the mass of the people by the minority who had the power and could employ lawyers and parliament to legalise that robbery. Without land of their own, long established by use and custom, the common people were now entirely dependent on someone to hire them for work or service for a wage, usually paid by the day or week. This produced a 'dependency culture' and the subservience so often condemned by the very people whose ancestors created and who themselves perpetuate it. It produces what Wilhelm Reich, Erich Fromm and others have described as the 'fascist character structure', the character which needs to have someone to tell it what to do, how to behave and what to believe.

So modern industrial nations are made up of a mass of people who can only, if asked, give opinions that have been made for them by the mass media. Dictatorships would be impossible without such a relationship between the leaders and the led. The image derives from the 'fasces', the symbol of authority in Rome – a bundle of rods held together with straps and carried by the lictor who, with those same rods, administered floggings when ordered to do so. The symbol also implies that without straps to hold them together as a unity, the rods would fall into a disorganised heap. Thus authority justified its use of unquestioned power. The irony is that 'identification' or the tendency to cause people to cooperate can develop a brutal and vicious face at need when the authority indicates to the mass media that some minorities, whether of race, politics or culture are persona non grata, as when black people in Britain were brought in by Enoch Powell and then harrassed for 'taking our jobs' when unemployment rose.

During industrial disputes between management and men this identification can be seen when secretaries, clerks and typists take the side of the employers even when their salaries and conditions of employment would make it reasonable for them to side with the men. Part of the problem in such cases has to do with the thesis formulated by Basil Bernstein concerning the assumed 'superiority' of what he calls 'the elaborated code' of language usage.

Up to this point – or down to it, if we are thinking in terms of status and power – language forms one of the ligaments that binds the different layers of the non-manual group together in the role of directing and controlling the economy. Literacy, at its most basic level, is essential to the co-ordinated working of the whole non-manual group. Those at the bottom of the hierarchy of control – the audio-typists, filing clerks, personal assistants, Girl Fridays or Dogsbodies (often the girlfriends, wives, sisters or daughters of men on the shop floor) find themselves torn between their loyalty to the boss and their understandable interest in the welfare of the firm, their employer on the one hand, and their loyalty to family and home culture on the other. For that reason they are often the target of overtly sexual advances by various levels of the boss group who feel, probably with good reason, that the girls identify with them and the business only at a superficial level and that to obviate any form of industrial espionage/sabotage they had better 'butter them up' with small presents, occasional dinners/drinks and cuddles at the office party.

But once you cross the threshold between management and shop floor the atmosphere changes. There need be no lack of politeness or even of cheerful banter between master and men; there may even be common canteens and toilets a la Japonaise, but the change in ambience is unmistakable. This is where skill with tools makes money and everybody knows it. Here the linguistic differences are palpable. Speech may be impossible because of the din of the machinery but the work goes on, or it may take the form of a single word, a brief phrase or a gesture. There are large areas of silence or of talk that has nothing to do with the work in hand: jokes, football, the dogs, fishing. But then, if so many of the jobs are repetitive, or but slight variations on an already well-known theme, what can be said that can maintain the original joy of the first work experience or express a burst of ecstasy on stamping out the three millionth paper clip? Alan Sillitoe's *Saturday Night and Sunday Morning* brilliantly captures the reactions of the factory-worker to the pattern of life that he will have to undergo for the fifty or so years of his working life. The relentless monotony and the virtual isolation drive him into a round of sexual fantasy that lasts while he is occupied in the mindless series of movements demanded by his machine. What else – or more pleasurable – can he do? His state education has not equipped him to analyse his position in society. What, certainly throughout history, he has often done is to devise new methods of doing the task before him, but whether he goes on doing that will depend on how the management receives his suggestions.

Language is both the product and the lifeblood of social action. It is so intimately part of our individuality that our friends can instantly recognise our voice from among those thousands of their acquaintances. In the form of thought it becomes a continuous dialogue with oneself and one's past experiences during any activity that is not of a purely routine nature. It is the vital basis to an intelligent awareness of the environment. It is the medium of community and the sap of culture. A human being without language is unthinkable. So the Industrial Revolution and the steady erosion of human intelligence from the work done by ordinary people can only be classified as the murder of humanity.

The Production Line
Let me set out in some detail why I make what may seem to be a rash assertion by considering work done under two different sets of conditions. The work to be done is the assembly of all the parts required to make a small truck to be used in Ethiopia for the relief of famine. In the first case the truck is assembled in a motor factory not yet equipped with robots and computer control, but with the usual production-line sytem that is largely still with us. In this system the whole layout of the factory and the movements of the workers have been designed in such a way that the raw materials and component parts move logically towards the end of the process – the finished product. The tools and the actions have been designed by time-and-motion studies so that each tool is made to do a specific job and so that no energy is wasted by the worker in doing it.

The same principle applies whether we are looking at one of the ancillary lines whch assemble and feed in to the main production line the various components such as frame, wheels, carburettor, fuel tank, bonnet. The order in which the components are fed to the main line is planned so as most conveniently to be assembled vis-a-vis other parts. At the same time and at the same rate the documentation relating to each vehicle passes through the system of administration in similar fashion. Nothing is overlooked; nothing is allowed to 'clog up the works'. Even the time taken for the various layers of paint to dry is worked into the programme. Nothing is left to chance: working shifts, dinner-breaks, tea-breaks are planned; unscheduled visits to the loo are frowned on. The human element is kept to a minimum because human beings are, at best, unpredictable and, at worst, positively dangerous since their inclination not to work 'flat out' is a main cause of lost profits. So long as within the system there is a need for thought or any doubt about what to do next there will be trouble in the essential sense that production will slow down. The man who attaches the wheels to the hubs cannot be trusted to put them on with the correct tension on the nuts. The planners therefore designed an air-driven torque spanner so adjusted that when the correct pressure was reached the friction clutch in the spanner slipped and ceased to turn the nut.

In such ways the possibility of human error, mischief or creativity was steadily eliminated from the production line. With error went thought, judgement and creativity on the part of the man on the shop floor. He was being dehumanised by work as effectively as if he were a part of the machine, firmly bolted on to it as an appendage.

The D-I-Y Method

Now let us take the example of a truck assembled under different conditions. A class of mature students studying economics and geography have become concerned with the problem of famine and evidently want to do something about it. We persuade a benevolent vehicle manufacturer to give us a truck to be sent to Ethiopia but the director cannot afford a completed truck. He sends us several crates containing all the parts that would make a complete truck and challenges us to assemble it. He lends us a large shed in which to work. How do we set about the task? None of the class is an engineer or a mechanic although several have done odd D-I-Y jobs on their own cars. As teacher I refrain from making decisions about how they should begin. Several suggest unpacking the crates to see what is inside and start to open one or two and spread the contents on the floor. Others protest and demand a discussion first. This is agreed and during the course of the discussion someone points out that as there are probably thousands of pieces in the crates we should make out some kind of plan. Someone then suggests a manual of the vehicle; someone else offers to get books about the vehicle assembly from the public library. After it is found that each crate contains a list of parts the class began to realise just how many pieces of metal, rubber, glass, plastic, brass they will have to deal with.

The following weeks and months was a trying time. Some quickly became bored and had to be nagged into fulfilling their promise; some were almost completely ignorant of basic principles of physics and needed much explanation; others showed a quick grasp of quite intricate components and explained them to others; some obviously understood but could not easily explain their meaning to others. By the end of the second week we began to see important differences in character. All quickly found that it was important to stop and think before attempting any job and would search thoroughly for any book that could help them. As a result of fitting various components and then finding that they had to remove them before they could fit others they began to think ahead more often. Throughout the whole period there was constant talk and argument about whether this should go before that or whether this was the right way to connect wires or pipes. Most of them began to spend time between classes reading about combustion engines or talking to motor engineers if they could find them.

The truck was finished in just under a year, having had the various layers of paint applied by brush since we could not get the use of a spray shop. The class, having arranged through Oxfam to get the truck shipped to Ethiopia, then arranged to visit the assembly shops of the firm that had given us the parts to make the truck. They found it a very sobering experience, their feelings being summed up in the statement 'What a deadly boring job to have to do day after day, week after week and year after year!' 'Aye. It's better than being wi'out job at all', was the reply of one older man.

When, shortly afterwards I tried to arrange for a visit by the class to the assembly shop in a factory that used robots I found a great reluctance on the part of the management. A few students might be allowed a brief visit to look at the shop floor from the supervisor's office. Their reaction after the visit was simply, 'What is going to be done with skilled workers if the computer is applied to more and more work of this kind? Surely the time is coming, has come already, for an assessment, on a national scale, of our future demands for workers of all types?'. The discussions that arose during the next few weeks ranged over the topics that are the stock-in-trade of the Green movement – dwindling resources, pollution, nuclear versus other forms of power – that take us beyond the scope of this paper. What had come clearly through their experience of building the truck was that it had made much wider demands on them than usual simply as people and on their power to express themselves, to solve problems along with others, to think and plan ahead.

Out of these questions arose others as the students reflected on the various kinds of work they had been trained to do and on the education that had preceded that work. It led them to undertake a broad survey of the system of education and its relation to the system of work as they knew it. That survey, made by reading, asking questions and reflecting on their own experiences forms the basis of what follows.

3
Education

For several months during the first year one of the students had been undergoing a course in psychotherapy, specifically psychoanalysis. For a long time he had not spoken about it, but as we had discussed the effects of mechanisation and of the whole system of mass-production on the people within it he began to speak about his experience of analysis and its effect on the ideas he had hitherto taken for granted. In the essay he wrote he started by describing in some detail the organisation of the factory and minute-by-minute movements of the man on the production line whom he had chosen. Then he went on:

'Important issues affecting the production of cars, such as the state of the economy or the international exchange rate or the balance of payments do not touch him through his work, though they touch him as he finds that his wages buy less and less with a decline in the value of the pound. Decisions affecting every aspect of work life are taken by others – managers, directors, shareholders, bankers, politicians. These issues are not for him unless he is politically conscious and very literate. At no point does he see himself functioning as a member of a team but he knows full well that what he and his mates do is a coherent and integrated effort.'

He followed this with an analysis of Bill's (the name he gave to the man under study) part in his Trade Union and the brutal oversimplification that pressure of work and the disinterest of so many of his mates produced in discussions of their problems with management. Then he looked in some detail, in the light of what had been uncovered by his own analysis, at the effects of such work on the men:

'They are all thus alienated from the products of their skill and from one another by the isolation created both by noise and, more effectively by the very process of work specialisation. Inevitably, therefore, they become alienated from themselves. How does this happen? All men and women build up their concepts of themselves from the reactions of their fellows to what they do, at work as well as in their private lives. When what they are doing together has a social value of benefit to the general community rather than something for their own pleasure or personal gain, the esteem they can build up is very important. The criteria for judging value relate to the function of the object or service and not simply to the worker's own opinion, so criticism based on aptness to purpose has nothing of a personal element directed at the worker and can therefore be accepted without resentment.

But when the subdivision of labour is carried to such lengths that the worker has to be disgruntled, ill, drunk or blind to make a mistake; and when he is not a member of a cooperating team engaged on a common task with a social end in view, then he loses the self-regulating experience of collective work where purposes and techniques are open and interactive. He has no tangible standards against which to measure himself; no incentives to correct weaknesses or to offer strengths for the benefit of others. He can develop no sense of community. His behaviour, his judgements, his very view of himself are informed by no social interchange. He becomes lost, alienated in the final sense. His behaviour is likely, therefore, to become bizarre, undirected, 'neurotic'.

Later he concluded:

'How can he find himself again except, if he has the money, by going to a psychiatrist. And what then becomes of him since he can only return to the conditions that created his distemper. While the psychiatrist may be able to help the wealthy to rationalise their exploiting function it can offer nothing to the working classes whose function is to continue to be exploited. No individual can offer a cure, only the recasting of the whole society will give us back our health.'

Then we looked at the process of education. A survey of their own education by the class showed a predominance of Comprehensive schools, with three of the class having been to Grammar schools. A survey conducted among their friends and acquaintances that included streets in their own neighbourhoods produced a pattern much closer to the general finding of sociologists. The class summarised these as follows:

'It is clear that the process of education is closely related to the roles that people are likely to play within the society as a whole. It is obvious, for example, that the Grammar school and the Public school prepare very well for literary, scientific and mathematical careers or for careers that demand intellectual abilities whereas the old Modern schools or the lower streams of the Comprehensives do not. It is also obvious that teachers in Public and Grammar schools come more often from Oxford or Cambridge than do teachers in other schools; and that the proportion of teachers to pupils is much more favourable in schools for the elite than it is in state schools. Further the amount of time spent in formal education ranges from an average of something over eleven years in Comprehensive schools to over fourteen years for those in Grammar schools who do not go on to take 'A' levels, but to over fifteen years for those who do. If onto those figures you add the time spent in Further or Higher education then the figures for those from Grammar schools and Public schools rise to over seventeen years. This does not include professional training which may add as much as a further three years to the total.

Now when you place the spectrum of schools, with the Comprehensives on the left, the Grammar schools on the right, and the Public schools on the extreme right, the relationship of the education system to the work spectrum becomes immediately obvious: the system of education is organised to educate the different strata of society for their adult roles.'

– a fair summary of sociological findings.

Looked at in more detail those findings show that whereas the proportion of teachers holding university degrees has risen in the profession as a whole the rise came from the BEd degree (awarded at the end of a teacher training course) – a degree held in low esteem by those holding normal first degrees because they are held to be an 'easy option'. The highest proportion of degrees from Oxford and Cambridge are held within the traditional Public schools and the Direct Grant Grammar schools. The ordinary Grammar schools have some staff with Oxbridge degrees and a larger number from the older universities such as London, Durham, Manchester and so on. In Comprehensive schools the proportion of normal university degrees together with Post Graduate Certificates in Education, awarded after one year of post-graduate study in education together with supervised teaching practice, tends to be higher in schools situated in areas with large middle-class populations and lower in schools serving predominantly working-class districts. For teachers university degrees have the additional advantage that they increase the teacher's pay.

Teachers with good degrees in specialised subjects such as modern languages or mathematics gravitate towards schools where subjects are taken to 'A' level because additional payments are made for the teaching of such subjects and, in particular, for the teaching of Science and Maths. In order to attract such teachers Local Authorities award to certain schools a greater number of special payments for the teaching of specialised subjects. When I was Head of a Modern school the Grammar school in the same town, with exactly the same number of pupils as I had, had more than three times the number of special subject payments and more than three times the number of staff holding good degrees.

Further, because the grant of money available for a school during the school year is determined not by the number of pupils but by the number of Burnham Units accumulated by the pupils, and because as pupils grow older they attract more units, schools in middle-class districts accumulate many more points than schools in working-class districts where children tend to leave school as soon as possible in order to help with the household budget. Middle-class parents, aware of their own debt to education are usually more prepared to sacrifice in order to keep their children at school to get good qualifications. For these reasons the Grammar school had many more staff, many more staff with good degrees and twice as much money to spend on books and equipment as I had for almost exactly the same number of pupils. The average teacher/pupil ratio in my school was then 1 to 28 and in the Grammar school 1 to 13.5, with the obvious effect that the Grammar school pupil received at least twice as much personal attention in every lesson as the pupil in my school.

All this is hardly surprising since those who lay down the structures of our education system are the group at the right-hand end of the work spectrum, along with the Education Officers and their senior assistants and the Chairmen of Education Committees. They all come to their jobs already predisposed to repeat the patterns with which they have long been familiar. David Glass in his book *Social Mobility in Britain* pointed out that the percentage of those who move from the social class into which they have been born, into another during their lifetime was about seven, but that at the extreme ends of the spectrum it drops to zero – in other words, if you are at the bottom you have to be a genius to move upwards, but if you are at the top you will be kept there even if you are an idiot. But if you have been to a Grammar school your chances of rising in the social scale are increased to the maximum. Every society sets up the system of education that reflects its values and that will per-petuate those values well into the future. So the poor are educated just to the point of being useful as factory-fodder while the rich are educated to make wealth and to hold on to the power that keeps them where they are – a crude enough formulation, but one that is bitterly true.

In discussing the 'charm', 'reasonableness' and 'confi-dence' of the British ruling class I undertook to look later at how these characteristics are developed. First it is impor-tant to realise that this class does not soil its hands with anything resembling manual work of any type done by servants. From infancy they are brought up by servants and may often develop a closer relatinship with Nanny than with mother, as Lord Edward Boyle, formerly Tory Minister of Education, told my wife and myself. As a Minister he was unusually sensitive to the need to make education as effective for all classes as possible and showed an unusual grasp, for that period, of the nature of intelligence and the fact that could be increased by suitable upbringing and education. In the film of L.P. Hartley's book *The Go-Between*, a sensitive study of a love-affair between a tenant-farmer and the daughter of the 'big house', the relationships between the gentry and their servants and employees are delicately drawn. The boys rush into the house scattering clothes as they go. Maid servants demurely pick up the clothes and tidy the rooms without thought of rebuke or complaint. When the family goes to the lake to bathe the young farmer is already there and tells them that he will have just one more 'header' before leaving. The boy graciously allows him to continue and then points out to the rest of the family how kind and polite he was in his behaviour to a servant. But when the liaison with the daughter is discovered the young farmer is expected to act so as not to embarrass either the daughter or the family. He does, by blowing his brains out.

A study of boarding-school education by Royston Lambert, *The Chance of a Lifetime?*, included 26 Public schools in its scope. The following passage condenses many of his findings about Public schools:

Eighty-one out of eighty-six Public schools are denominational, mostly Church of England. they seek to make boys become responsible, tolerant, intellectually competent, physically healthy and Christian leaders – the 'Arnold tradition'. Because they form a closed society the goals and values of the school are clear and strong. Governing bodies obviously influence the goals of schools. They are often as much concerned with expressive matters; their Governors, mostly educated in the same schools, reinforce their ethos. In some religious schools the staff and the governing body are largely the same people exercising different roles as in an Oxbridge college. Their former pupils are usually gathered into elaborate organisations, almost sub-cultures, with premises, officials, periodicals, insignia and rituals of their own. They serve to maintain the stress on continuity and can provide invaluable support for the school financially and in penetrating other bodies: employers, colleges, local authorities and the like.

Public schools sometimes possess their own junior or infants' departments so that the integration with their ethos can start at three or six years of age and last until eighteen. . . [see above the 'old boy' network. M.D.]. The Headmasters' Conference exists as a public relations body, highly selective, to maintain a consensus on goals, standards and methods while government educational policy has had little effect on them: they still remain outside the pattern of national education despite two government enquiries into the matter.

Between them and the older universities of Oxford and Cambridge there exists a special relationship [with] over eighty-two percent of the school's staff and more of their governors [as] alumni of Oxford or Cambridge. . .

Though the proportion of Public school boarders entering Oxbridge is declining and the older universities regard their traditional link with the Public schools with some unease nowadays, the proportion of Public school boarders entering Oxford and Cambridge is still greater than their share of the total numbers entering all universities would normally warrant: fifty-five percent of public school boarders going to university enter Oxbridge, compared with thirteen percent leaving all state grammar schools. Various professions, the diplomatic corps, the higher ranks of the civil service, judges and barristers, the episcopate, city business companies and financiers still come largely from Public school. The connection between them is, however, not specific: the schools prepare for this high *level* or *grade* of employment by providing the necessary general culture, the requisite cognitive or emotional patterns.

When a boy enters Public schools he comes from a home where the care of the boy has been delegated over a wide area to servants and where most of his time since the age of eight will have been spent in a single-sex school which prepares him specifically for Public school. By the time he reaches adolescence there is an inhibition on expressing feelings and "a tendency towards more strained relations with affective figures such as the mother".

Most teachers in Public schools come from social groups which correspond to those of their pupils: the higher socio-economic groupings and the majority of staff tend to come from families already established in such groups. Over seventy percent of staff in Public schools were themselves educated at Public schools and about ten percent of them were educated in their own school.

With such a network of cohesive factors shaping the character and personality of the public school boy and having spent so long without the unconditional love tht any normal child receives at home it is no wonder that he is a highly armoured personality, seeks to embroil himself tightly within the social culture towards those of different cultures, disguised often as wary politeness. The implicit embargo on emotional expression and his virtual isolation from girls renders him vulnerable not only to those who want to take advantage of him but to his own emotions.

Like all profiles produced from sociological studies the image that results is a generality, a trend. Exceptions occur that vary on both sides of the mean. Some Public school products are exceptionaly warm and creative people, for whatever reasons. What is, however, a matter of concern, in view of the positions of power they occupy in our society, is a very common tendency to formulate policies that are over-rigid and inadequately sensitive to the needs of those outside their culture or class. In the highly centralised, over-administered and over-populated society that is Britain at the end of the twentieth century such over-strung and dog-matic propensities need cautious handling. It becomes even more urgent to extend democratic forms and procedures more broadly throughout our society as a protection against dictatorial habits that have been growing since the war and more rapidly during the last two decades.

But, since no dictatorship can long exist if the majority of its citizens have the confidence to exercise their collective will, it is even more imporant to bring all our children up from infancy in a democratic milieu, giving them the experi-ence of making decisions over matters that affect them, as the children at A.S. Neill's school, Summerhill, have always done. Democracy, like language, needs practice from infancy if it is to become as much part of our natures as language is.

MICHAEL DUANE, 1991